Table of Contents

Rourke
Educational Media
rourkeeducationalmedia.com

Can you find these words?

circle

oval

spiral

triangle

Shapes in Nature

Nature is full of shapes.

There is an orange tree. Yummy!

circle

An orange is a **circle** shape.

A slimy snail moves slowly.

A snail's shell is a **spiral** shape.

spiral

Look at the starfish.

It is a star shape.

Birds peck at seeds on the ground.

The bird's beak is a **triangle** shape.

triangle

Lemons grow on trees.
They are sour!

oval

They are an **oval** shape.

Did you find these words?

An orange is a **circle** shape.

Lemons are sour. They are an **oval** shape.

A snail's shell is a **spiral** shape.

The bird's beak is a **triangle** shape.

Photo Glossary

 **circle** (SUR-kuhl): A round shape, like the shape of an orange.

 **oval** (OH-vuhl): Something that is shaped like an egg or a lemon.

 **spiral** (SPYE-ruhl): A shape that winds in a continuous curve, like a snail's shell.

 **triangle** (TRYE-ayn-guhl): A shape with three sides and three angles.

Index

About the Author

Pete Jenkins loves to take long walks outside and look at all the interesting shapes found in nature. He lives by the ocean where there are many wonderful shapes to be found.

www.rourkeeducationalmedia.com

PHOTO CREDITS: Cover: ©vencavolrab; p.2,4-5,14,15: ©ChrisBoswell; p.2,12-13,14,15: ©odmeyer; p.2,6-7,14,15: ©ayurara; p.2,10-11,14,15: ©Kewuwu I Dreamstime.com; p.3: ©bgfoto; p.8: ©Damsea

Edited by: Keli Sipperley
Cover and interior design by: Rhea Magaro-Wallace

Library of Congress PCN Data
Shapes in Nature / Pete Jenkins
(I Know)
ISBN (hard cover)(alk. paper) 978-1-64156-171-6
ISBN (soft cover) 978-1-64156-227-0
ISBN (e-Book) 978-1-64156-280-5
Library of Congress Control Number: 2017957781

Printed in the United States of America, North Mankato, Minnesota